ISBN: 9781314502916

Published by:
HardPress Publishing
8345 NW 66TH ST #2561
MIAMI FL 33166-2626

Email: info@hardpress.net
Web: http://www.hardpress.net

JOHN HENRY NASH LIBRARY
❖ SAN FRANCISCO ❖
PRESENTED TO THE
UNIVERSITY OF CALIFORNIA
ROBERT GORDON SPROUL, PRESIDENT.
❖ BY ❖
MR. AND MRS. MILTON S. RAY
CECILY, VIRGINIA AND ROSALYN RAY
AND THE
RAY OIL BURNER COMPANY
SAN FRANCISCO
NEW YORK

University of California · Berkeley

Paul Elder
Publisher

John Henry Nash
Printer

WESTERN CLASSICS
Nº THREE

TENNESSEE'S PARTNER

TENNESSEE'S PARTNER
BY BRET HARTE, INCLUDING
AN INTRODUCTION BY WILLIAM
DALLAM ARMES, THE FRONTISPIECE
IN PHOTOGRAVURE FROM A PAINTING
BY ALBERTINE RANDALL WHEELAN

PAUL ELDER AND COMPANY
SAN FRANCISCO AND NEW YORK

THE INTRODUCTION [i

¶ *When Marshall's discovery caused a sudden influx of thousands of adventurers from all classes and almost all countries, the conditions of government in California were almost the worst possible. Though the Mexican system was unpopular and the Mexican law practically unknown, until other provision was made by congress, they had to continue in force. But the free and slave states were equal in number; California would turn the scale; there was a battle royal as to which pan should descend, a battle that the congresses of 1848 and 1849 left unsettled on adjourning. ¶ Under these circumstances, it* might be supposed that the worst elements would get the upper hand, crime become common, and anarchy result. Precisely the opposite happened. The de facto government was accepted as a necessity, and under its direction "alcaldes" and "ayuntamientos" were elected. But the mining-camps, which were in a part of the country that had not been settled by the Mexicans and were occupied by men who knew nothing of their system or laws, were left to work out their own salvation. The preponderating element was the Anglo-Saxon, and its genius for law and order asserted itself. Each *camp elected its own officers, recognized the customary laws and adopted special ones, and punished lawbreakers. Naturally theft was considered a more serious crime than it is in ordinary communities. As there were no jails or jailors, flogging and expulsion were the usual punishment, but in aggravated cases it was death. Even after the state government had been organized, indeed, the law for a short while permitted a jury to prescribe the death penalty for grand larceny, and, in fact, several notorious thieves were legally executed. ¶ The testimony of all observers is that the camps were surprisingly orderly, that crime was infrequent, and that its punishment, though swift and certain, leaned to mercy rather than rigor. Bayárd Taylor, for example, who was in the mines in '50 and '51, writes: "In a region five hundred miles long, inhabited by a hundred thousand people, who had neither locks, bolts, regular laws of government, military or civil protection, there was as much security to life and property as in any state of the Union." ¶As these "miners' courts" were allowed after the organization of the state to retain jurisdiction in all questions that concerned the appropriation of claims,* the miners but slowly appreciated that they had been shorn of their criminal jurisdiction. But that they did come to recognize that "the old order changeth, yielding place to new," is, in fact, shown by the very incident on which Harte based his story of a lynching. ¶Spite of the autobiographic method that leads the casual reader to think that Harte was intimately connected with this early pioneer life and derived the material for his sketches from personal observation and experience, his is, in truth, only hearsay evidence. The heroic age was with Iram and all his rose ere he landed in 1854, a lad of eighteen. With no especial equipment for battling with the world, he had to turn his hand to many things, and naturally tried mining. But finding the returns incommensurate with the labor, he soon gave it up and sought more congenial occupations, mainly in the towns of the valleys and the seacoast. Before he was twenty-three, he had been school-teacher, express-messenger, deputy tax-collector, and druggist's assistant; and had risen from "printer's devil" to assistant editor of a country newspaper. In 1859 he was back in San Francisco, utilizing the trade he had picked *up, as a compositor on* The Golden Era. *To this he contributed poems and local sketches that soon led to his appointment as assistant editor. His writings made him friends, one of whom,* Thomas Starr King, *in 1864, obtained for him the position of secretary to the superintendent of the Mint. His duties were not arduous, and his rooms became the resort of his literary associates and of men from " the diggings," whose mines, like the meadows of Concord, yielded a two-fold crop: gold-dust for the superintendent to turn into bullion, and stories for his young secretary later to turn into literature. By*

1868 his reputation was so great that when Mr. A. Roman established The Overland Monthly, *he was made its first editor.* ¶ *Mr. Roman impressed upon him the literary possibilities of the life of the miners, and furnished him with incidents, tales, and pictures. " The Luck of Roaring Camp," his first venture in this hitherto almost untouched field, proved that Bret Harte had come into his own. His local sketches and Mexican legends had been imitative of Irving, his stories of Dickens; but for this he had evolved a method and a style distinctly personal. His first success was followed up by " The Outcasts* of Poker Flat" and (in October, 1869) by the tale here reprinted; and when, in 1870, an Eastern house published his sketches in book form, his fame was secure. In 1871 he left California, and after a few years in the East that added little to his reputation as a writer, or as a man, secured a consulate in Germany. In 1878 he left America forever. Till his death in 1902 he wrote on, frequently recurring to the claim where he first "got the color," but never equaling his work during the year and a half that he was editor of the Overland. ¶In 1866 Harte heard, from one who had been pres-

ent, the incident that inspired " Tennessee's Partner." Eleven years before, at Second Garrote, a newcomer had committed a capital crime. The miners organized a court, appointed counsel, and gave the miscreant a trial. He confessed his guilt, and the cry arose, " Hang him!" But " Old Man Chaffee" stepped forward, drew a bag of gold-dust from his bosom, and said that he would give his " pile" rather than have a lynching occur in a camp that, spite its name, had never been so disgraced. He begged the crowd to turn the prisoner over to the authorities and let the law take its course. Such was the fervor of his appeal and so great were the respect and affection for the old man that his proposal was adopted with a cheer for the advocate of law and order, and the culprit taken to the jail at Columbia. ¶ *Chaffee's partner, Chamberlain, seems to have had no part in this affair; but the two were united by a love like that of his partner for Tennessee. And long after the Second Garrote had become but a memory, the two octogenarians lived on in their little cabin, Chaffee seeking with primitive pick, shovel, and pan the more and more elusive gold, and Chamberlain contributing to the common purse by cultivating a small "ranch," the best crop of which was the campers who came to chat of bygone days with "the original of Tennessee's Partner." At last, in 1903, their partnership of fifty-four years was ended by the death of Chaffee. Within eight weeks he was followed by Chamberlain. Their last days were made easy by the bounty of Professor W. E. Magee, of the State University, to whom I am indebted for the authority for some of these statements,— Chamberlain's journal. ¶From this simple material the imagination of Bret Harte spun the characters, incidents,* and motives that his genius wove into an exquisite fabric, an idyl of blind, unreasoning love of man for man. He was not writing history; and the complaint of those who were part of the life he depicted, that he mis-stated the facts, rests on the same failure to appreciate his purpose and method that leads Eastern and English critics to consider his realism reality and to mistake his verisimilitude for the truth itself. The fact is that Bret Harte was a consummate literary artist, who used facts with all an artist's freedom. His genius "imbalm'd and treasur'd up on purpose to a life beyond life," however,

*many an actual incident that other-
wise would lie buried 'neath the
poppy that the iniquity of oblivion
blindly scattereth.*

WM. DALLAM ARMES.

TENNESSEE'S PARTNER

¶ I do not think that we ever knew his real name. Our ignorance of it certainly never gave us any social inconvenience, for at Sandy Bar in 1854 most men were christened anew. Sometimes these appellatives were derived from some distinctiveness of dress, as in the case of "Dungaree Jack"; or from some peculiarity of habit, as shown in "Saleratus Bill," so called from an undue proportion of that chemical in his daily bread; or from some unlucky slip, as exhibited in "The Iron Pirate," a mild, inoffensive man, who earned that baleful title by his unfortunate mispronunciation of the term "iron pyrites." Perhaps this may have been the beginning of a rude heraldry; but I am constrained to think that it was because a man's real name in that day rested solely upon his own unsupported statement. "Call yourself Clifford, do you?" said Boston, addressing a timid newcomer with infinite scorn; "hell is full of such Cliffords!" He then introduced the unfortunate man, whose name happened to be really Clifford, as "Jaybird Charley,"— an unhallowed inspiration of the moment that clung to him ever after. ¶But to return to Tennessee's Partner, whom we never knew by any other than this relative title; that he had ever existed as a separate and distinct individuality we only learned later. It seems that in 1853 he left Poker Flat to go to San Francisco, ostensibly to procure a wife. He never got any farther than Stockton. At that place he was attracted by a young person who waited upon the table at the hotel where he took his meals. One morning he said something to her which caused her to smile not unkindly, to somewhat coquettishly break a plate of toast over his upturned, serious, simple face, and to retreat to the kitchen. He followed her, and emerged a few moments later, covered with more toast and victory. That day week they were married by a Justice of the Peace, and returned to Poker Flat. I am aware that something more might be made of this episode, but I prefer to tell it as it was current at Sandy Bar,—in the gulches and barrooms,—where all sentiment was modified by a strong sense of humor. ¶Of their married felicity but little is known, perhaps for the reason that Tennessee, then living with his partner, one day took occasion to say something to the bride on his own account, at which, it is said, she smiled not unkindly, and chastely retreated,— this time as far as Marysville, where Tennessee followed her, and where they went to housekeeping without the aid of a Justice of the Peace. Tennessee's Partner took the loss of his wife simply and seriously, as was his fashion. But to everybody's surprise, when Tennessee one day returned from Marysville, without his partner's wife,—she having smiled and retreated with somebody else,—Tennessee's Partner was the first man to shake his hand and greet him with affection. The boys who had gathered in the cañon to see the shooting were naturally indignant. Their indignation might have found vent in sarcasm but for a certain look in Tennessee's Partner's eye that indicated a lack of humorous appreciation. In fact, he was a grave man, with a steady application to practical detail which was unpleasant in a difficulty. ¶ Meanwhile a popular feeling against Tennessee had grown up on the Bar. He was known to be a gambler; he was suspected to be a thief. In

these suspicions Tennessee's Partner was equally compromised; his
continued intimacy with Tennessee after the affair above quoted
could only be accounted for on the
hypothesis of a copartnership of
crime. At last Tennessee's guilt
became flagrant. One day he
overtook a stranger on his way to
Red Dog. The stranger afterward
related that Tennessee beguiled
the time with interesting anecdote
and reminiscence, but illogically
concluded the interview in the fol-
lowing words: "And now, young
man, I'll trouble you for your
knife, your pistols, and your money.

You see your weppings might get you into trouble at Red Dog, and your money's a temptation to the evilly disposed. I think you said your address' was San Francisco. I shall endeavor to call." It may be stated here that Tennessee had a fine flow of humor, which no business preoccupation could wholly subdue. ¶ This exploit was his last. Red Dog and Sandy Bar made common cause against the highwayman. Tennessee was hunted in very much the same fashion as his prototype, the grizzly. As the toils closed around him, he made a desperate dash

through the Bar, emptying his re-
volver at the crowd before the
Arcade Saloon, and so on up
Grizzly Cañon; but at its farther
extremity he was stopped by a
small man on a gray horse. The
men looked at each other a moment in silence. Both were fear-
less, both self-possessed and inde-
pendent, and both types of a
civilization that in the seventeenth
century would have been called
heroic, but in the nineteenth simply "reckless." "What have you
got there?—I call," said Tennessee, quietly. "Two bowers and
an ace," said the stranger, as

quietly, showing two revolvers and a bowie-knife. "That takes me," returned Tennessee; and, with this gambler's epigram, he threw away his useless pistol, and rode back with his captor. ¶ It was a warm night. The cool breeze which usually sprang up with the going down of the sun behind the chaparral-crested mountain was that evening withheld from Sandy Bar. The little cañon was stifling with heated resinous odors, and the decaying driftwood on the Bar sent forth faint, sickening exhalations. The feverishness of day and its fierce passions still filled the camp. Lights moved restlessly along the bank of the river, striking no answering reflection from its tawny current. Against the blackness of the pines the windows of the old loft above the express-office stood out staringly bright; and through their curtainless panes, the loungers below could see the forms of those who were even then deciding the fate of Tennessee. And above all this, etched on the dark firmament, rose the Sierra, remote and passionless, crowned with remoter passionless stars. ¶The trial of Tennessee was conducted as fairly as was consistent with a judge and jury who felt themselves to some extent obliged to justify, in their verdict, the previous irregularities of arrest and indictment. The law of Sandy Bar was implacable, but not vengeful. The excitement and personal feeling of the chase were over; with Tennessee safe in their hands they were ready to listen patiently to any defense, which they were already satisfied was insufficient. There being no doubt in their own minds, they were willing to give the prisoner the benefit of any that might exist. Secure in the hypothesis that he ought to be hanged, on general principles, they indulged him with more latitude of defense than his reckless hardihood seemed to ask. The Judge appeared to be more anxious than the prisoner, who, otherwise unconcerned, evidently took a grim pleasure in the responsibility he had created. "I don't take any hand in this yer game," had been his invariable but good-humored reply to all questions. The Judge—who was also his captor—for a moment vaguely regretted that he had not shot him "on sight," that morning, but presently dismissed this human weakness as unworthy of the judicial mind. Nevertheless, when there was a tap at the door, and it was said that Tennessee's Partner was there on behalf of the prisoner, he was admitted at once without question. Perhaps the younger members of the jury, to whom the proceedings were becoming irksomely thoughtful, hailed him as a relief. ¶For he was not, certainly, an imposing figure. Short and stout, with a square face, sunburned into a preternatural redness, clad in a loose duck "jumper" and trousers streaked and splashed with red soil, his aspect under any circumstances would have been quaint, and was now even ridiculous. As he stooped to deposit at his feet a heavy carpet-bag he was carrying, it became obvious, from partially developed legends and inscriptions, that the material with which his trousers had been patched had been originally intended for a less ambitious covering. Yet he advanced with great gravity, and after shaking the hand of each person in the room with labored cordiality, he wiped his serious, perplexed face on a red bandanna handkerchief, a shade lighter than his complexion, laid his powerful hand upon the table to steady himself, and thus addressed the Judge:—"I was passin' by," he began, by way of apology, "and I thought I'd just step in and see how things was gittin' on with Tennessee thar,— my pardner. It's a hot night. I disremember any sich weather before on the Bar." ¶He paused a moment, but nobody volunteering any other meteorological recollection, he again had recourse to his pocket-handkerchief, and for some moments mopped his face diligently. ¶"Have you anything to say on behalf of the prisoner?" said the Judge, finally. ¶ "Thet's it," said Tennessee's Partner, in a tone of relief. "I come yar as Tennessee's pardner,—knowing him nigh on four year, off and on, wet and dry, in luck and out o' luck. His ways ain't allers my ways, but thar ain't any p'ints in that young man, thar ain't any liveliness as he's been up to, as I don't know. And you sez to me, sez you,— confidential-like, and between man and man,—sez you, 'Do you know anything in his behalf?' and I sez to you, sez I,— confidential-like, as between man and man,—'What should a man know of his pardner?'" ¶ "Is this all you have to say?" asked the Judge impatiently, feeling, perhaps, that a dangerous sympathy of humor was beginning to humanize the court. ¶ "Thet's so," continued Tennessee's Partner. "It ain't for me to say anything agin' him. And now, what's the case? Here's Tennessee wants money, wants it bad, and doesn't like to ask it of his old pardner. Well, what does Tennessee do? He lays for a stranger, and he fetches that stranger; and you lays for *him,* and you fetches *him;* and the honors is easy. And I put it to you, bein' a far-minded man, and to you, gentlemen all, as far-minded men, ef this isn't so." ¶ "Prisoner," said the Judge, interrupting, "have you any questions to ask this man?" ¶ "No! no!" continued Tennessee's Partner hastily. "I play this yer hand alone. To come down to the bed-rock, it's just this: Tennessee, thar, has played it pretty rough and expensive-like on a stranger, and on this yer camp. And now, what's the fair thing? Some would say more; some would say less. Here's seventeen hundred dollars in coarse gold and a watch,—it's about all my pile,—and call it square!" And before a hand could be raised to prevent him, he had emptied the contents of the carpet-bag upon the table. ¶ For a moment his life was in jeopardy. One or two men sprang to their feet, several hands groped for hidden weapons, and a suggestion to "throw him from the window," was only overridden by a gesture from the Judge. Tennessee laughed. And apparently oblivious of the excitement, Tennessee's Partner improved the opportunity to mop his face again with his handkerchief. ¶ When order was restored, and the man was made to understand, by the use of forcible figures and rhetoric, that Tennessee's offense could not be condoned by money, his face took a more serious and sanguinary hue, and those who were nearest to him noticed that his rough hand trembled slightly on the table. He hesitated a moment as he slowly returned the gold to the carpet-bag, as if he had not yet entirely caught the elevated sense of justice which swayed the tribunal, and was perplexed with the belief that he had not offered enough. Then he turned to the Judge, and saying, "This yer is a lone hand, played alone, and without my pardner," he bowed to the jury and was about to withdraw, when the Judge called him back. "If you have anything to say to Tennessee, you had better say it now." For the first time that evening the eyes of the prisoner and his strange advocate met. Tennessee smiled, showed his white teeth, and saying, "Euchred, old man!" held out his hand. Tennessee's Partner took it in his own, and saying, "I just dropped in as I was passin' to see how things was gettin' on," let the hand passively fall, and adding that "it was a warm night," again mopped his face with his handkerchief, and without another word withdrew. ¶ The two men never again met each other alive. For the unparalleled insult of a bribe offered to Judge Lynch — who, whether bigoted, weak, or narrow, was at least incorruptible — firmly fixed in the mind of that mythical personage any wavering determination of Tennessee's fate; and at the break of day he was marched, closely guarded, to meet it at the top of Marley's Hill. ¶ How he met it, how cool he was, how he refused to say anything, how perfect were the arrangements of the committee, were all duly reported, with the addition of a warning moral and example to all future evil-doers, in the Red Dog *Clarion*, by its editor, who was present, and to whose vigorous English I cheerfully refer the reader. But the beauty of that midsummer morning, the blessed amity of earth and air and sky, the awakened life of the free woods and hills, the joyous renewal and promise of Nature, and, above all, the infinite serenity that thrilled through each, was not reported, as not being a part of the social lesson. And yet, when the weak and foolish deed was done, and a life, with its possibilities and responsibilities, had passed out of the misshapen thing that dangled between earth and sky, the birds sang, the flowers bloomed, the sun shone, as cheerily as before; and possibly the Red Dog *Clarion* was right. ¶ Tennessee's Partner was not in the group that surrounded the ominous tree. But as they turned to disperse, attention was drawn to the singular appearance of a motionless donkey-cart halted at the side of the road. As they approached, they at once recognized the venerable Jenny and the two-wheeled cart as the property of Tennessee's Partner,—used by him in carrying dirt from his claim; and a few paces distant, the owner of the equipage himself, sitting under a buckeye tree, wiping the perspiration from his glowing face. In answer to an inquiry, he said he had come for the body of the "diseased," "if it was all the same to the committee." He did n't wish to "hurry anything"; he could wait. He was not working that day; and when the gentlemen were done with the "diseased" he would take him. "Ef thar is any present," he added, in his simple, serious way, "as would care to jine in the fun'l, they kin come." Perhaps it was from a sense of humor, which I have already intimated was a feature of Sandy Bar,—perhaps it was from something even better than that; but two-thirds of the loungers accepted the invitation at once. ¶ It was noon when the body of Tennessee was delivered into the hands of his partner. As the cart drew up to the fatal tree, we noticed that it contained a rough oblong box,—apparently made from a section of sluicing,—and half filled with bark and the tassels of pine. The cart was further decorated with slips of willow, and made fragrant with buckeye-blossoms. When the body was deposited in the box, Tennessee's Partner drew over it a piece of tarred canvas, and gravely mounting the narrow seat in front, with his feet upon the shafts, urged the little donkey forward. The equipage moved slowly on, at that decorous pace which was habitual with Jenny even under less solemn circumstances. The men — half curiously, have jestingly, but all good-humoredly — strolled along beside the cart; some in advance, some a little in the rear, of the homely catafalque. But, whether from the narrowing of the road or some present sense of decorum, as the cart passed on, the company fell to the rear in couples, keeping step, and otherwise assuming the external show of a formal procession. Jack Folinsbee, who had at the outset played a funeral march in dumb show upon an imaginary trombone, desisted, from a lack of sympathy and appreciation,—not having, perhaps, your true humorist's capacity to be content with the enjoyment of his own fun.

¶ The way led through Grizzly Cañon, by this time clothed in funereal drapery and shadows. The redwoods, burying their moccasined feet in the red soil, stood in Indian-file along the track, trailing an uncouth benediction from their bending boughs upon the passing bier. A hare, surprised into helpless inactivity, sat upright and pulsating in the ferns by the roadside, as the *cortège* went by. Squirrels hastened to gain a secure outlook from higher boughs; and the blue-jays, spreading their wings, fluttered before them like outriders, until the outskirts of Sandy Bar were reached, and the solitary cabin of Tennessee's Partner. ¶ Viewed under more favorable circumstances, it would not have been a cheerful place. The un-picturesque site, the rude and unlovely outlines, the unsavory details, which distinguish the nest-building of the California miner, were all here, with the dreariness of decay superadded. A few paces from the cabin there was a rough enclosure, which, in the brief days of Tennessee's Partner's matri-monial felicity, had been used as a garden, but was now overgrown with fern. As we approached it we were surprised to find that what we had taken for a recent attempt at cultivation was the broken soil about an open grave. ¶ The cart was halted before the enclosure; and rejecting the offers of assistance with the same air of simple self-reliance he had displayed throughout, Tennessee's Partner lifted the rough coffin on his back, and deposited it, unaided, within the shallow grave. He then nailed down the board which served as a lid, and, mounting the little mound of earth beside it, took off his hat, and slowly mopped his face with his handkerchief. This the crowd felt was a preliminary to speech; and they disposed themselves variously on stumps and boulders, and sat expectant. ¶ "When a man," began Tennessee's Partner slowly, "has been running free all day, what's the natural thing for him to do? Why, to come home. And if he ain't in a condition to go home, what can his best friend do? Why, bring him home! And here's Tennessee has been running free, and we brings him home from his wandering." He paused, and picked up a fragment of quartz, rubbed it thoughtfully on his sleeve, and went on: "It ain't the first time that I've packed him on my back, as you see'd me now. It ain't the first time that I brought him to this yer cabin when he could n't help himself; it ain't the first time that I and Jinny have waited for him on yon hill, and picked him up and so fetched him home, when he could n't speak, and did n't know me. And now that it's the last time, why"—he paused, and rubbed the quartz gently on his sleeve—"you see it's sort of rough on his pardner. And now, gentlemen," he added abruptly, picking up his long-handled shovel, "the fun'l's over; and my thanks, and Tennessee's thanks, to you for your trouble." ¶ Resisting any proffers of assistance, he began to fill in the grave, turning his back upon the crowd, that, after a few moments' hesitation, gradually withdrew. As they crossed the little ridge that hid Sandy Bar from view, some, looking back, thought they could see Tennessee's Partner, his work done, sitting upon the grave, his shovel between his knees, and his face buried in his red bandanna handkerchief. But it was argued by others that you could n't tell his face from his handkerchief at that distance; and this point remained undecided. ¶ In the reaction that followed the feverish excitement of that day, Tennessee's Partner was not forgotten. A secret investigation had cleared him of any complicity in Tennessee's guilt, and left only a suspicion of his general sanity. Sandy Bar made a point of calling on him, and proffering various uncouth but well-meant kindnesses. But from that day his rude health and great strength seemed visibly to decline; and when the rainy season fairly set in, and the tiny grass-blades were beginning to peep from the rocky mound above Tennessee's grave, he took to his bed. ¶ One night, when the pines beside the cabin were swaying in the storm, and trailing their slender fingers over the roof, and the roar and rush of the swollen river were heard below, Tennessee's Partner lifted his head from the pillow, saying, "It is time to go for Tennessee; I must put Jinny in the cart;" and would have risen from his bed but for the restraint of his attendant. Struggling, he still pursued his singular fancy: "There, now, steady, Jinny,—steady, old girl. How dark it is! Look out for the ruts,—and look out for him, too, old gal. Sometimes, you know, when he's blind drunk, he drops down right in the trail. Keep on straight up to the pine on the top of the hill. Thar! I told you so!—thar he is,—coming this way, too,—all by himself, sober, and his face a-shining. Tennessee! Pardner!" ¶ And so they met.

HERE ENDS Nº THREE OF THE WESTERN
CLASSICS, BEING TENNESSEE'S PARTNER
BY BRET HARTE, THE INTRODUCTION BY
WILLIAM DALLAM ARMES. THE PHOTO-
GRAVURE FRONTISPIECE BY ALBERTINE
RANDALL WHEELAN. OF THIS FIRST
EDITION ONE THOUSAND COPIES HAVE
BEEN ISSUED, PRINTED UPON FABRIANO
HANDMADE PAPER. THE TYPOGRAPHY
DESIGNED BY J. H. NASH. PUBLISHED
BY PAUL ELDER AND COMPANY, AND
DONE INTO A BOOK FOR THEM AT THE
TOMOYE PRESS, NEW YORK CITY, IN THE
YEAR NINETEEN HUNDRED AND SEVEN

ImTheStory.com

CPSIA information can be obtained at www.ICGtesting.com
Printed in the USA
BVOW08s1213040814

361596BV00036B/1418/P